© Copyright, 2023, Author

All rights reserved. No part of this book may be reproduced, stored in a retrieval system, or transmitted, in any form by any means, electronic, mechanical, magnetic, optical, chemical, manual, photocopying, recording or otherwise, without the prior written consent of its writer.

Price: Rs. 350/-

The opinions/ contents expressed in this book are solely of the author and do not represent the opinions/ standings/ thoughts of Publisher.

Printed in India

PRACTICAL MANUAL
for
Department of Agricultural Economics

Semester: VI
Course Name: Farm Management, Production, and Resource Economics
Course Code: ECON – 365
Credit   : 2 (1 + 1)

Prepared By:
Dr. Neha Dwivedi
Dr. Veena Rathore
Dr. Savita Chouhan

INDEX

© Copyright, 2023, Author

Exercise No. 1
BASIC CONCEPTS AND TERMINOLOGIES IN FARM MANAGEMENT
AND AGRICULTURAL PRODUCTION ECONOMICS

1. **Farm** - The smallest unit of agriculture is called a farm, and it can be made up of one or more plots farmed by a single farmer or by a group of farmers together to raise livestock and crops. It functions as a producing and consuming unit simultaneously.

2. **Family Farm** - In brief, a family holding (farm) can be described as being comparable, depending on the local circumstances and current technical conditions, to either a plough unit or a work unit for a family of average size.

3. **Agriculture** - Agriculture is the culmination of all agricultural production methods and livestock-rearing techniques used on a single Farm.

4. **Farm firm** -. A farm holding is an example of an economic unit. It is a production unit that is managed. The term "economic unit" also refers to an aggregate of resources for which costs and returns are calculated collectively.

5. **Technical unit** - A technical unit alludes to a single, convenient unit in production for which technical coefficients are computed e.g. an acre of land, a cow, a unit of poultry birds, etc. It is an exact single unit in production.

6. **Farm Plant** - It is a collection of technical units e.g. 5 a mixed farm or a dairy farm.

7. **Economic unit** - It is the sum of resources for which costs, returns, and net income can be worked out.

   Synonyms -

   i) Factors of production/resources/inputs.

   ii) Factor-product relationship / input-output relationship/input responses.

8. **Resources** - During the production process, certain inputs or resources—such as water, fertilizers, and insecticides—are used up or converted into finished goods. Certain resources, including labour, tools, and structures, are only available as services that can be turned into products.

   i) Stock and flow inputs.

   ii) Combination of stock and flow services (continuous inputs and discontinuous inputs).

1

9. **Fixed and variable resources -** Regardless of the scale of the enterprises undertaken, the resources, such as farm buildings, machinery, and implements, are fixed throughout a planning period. We refer to these as fixed farm resources.

Variable resources are those whose utilization fluctuates accordingly on an enterprise's level; examples include seed and feed. Certain permanent resources, such as bullock labour, tractor services, etc., are also used as variable resources.

10. **Production in Transformation period -** It is the interval of time between efforts and returns. It is the process of turning specific service resources into finished goods.

11. **Production function -** The relationship between an independent variable (input), and the dependent variable (output) can be referred to as a production function. It is a technical and mathematical relationship describing the extent to which a particular product depends upon the quantities of inputs or services of inputs used. Forms of production function or ways of representing preparation of farm.

1) Tabular form
2) Algebraic form
3) Graphic form

Exercise No. 2
TO STUDY LAW OF RETURNS

Laws of returns refer to the amount of output secured by the addition of variable input to fixed inputs. There are three types of laws of returns (Input-Output relationship) in the production of a commodity, where one input varies and the quantities of all other inputs are fixed. The relationship between the input of a single variable factor and the output of a single product can be either one or the combinations of types given below.

1. Law of constant returns or constant marginal productivity.

2. Law of increasing returns or increasing marginal productivity.

3. Law of diminishing returns or decreasing marginal productivity.

A) Law of Constant returns

Here each additional unit of the variable input when applied to the fixed factor produces an equal amount of additional product i.e. the amount of total product increases by the same magnitude or at a constant rate per unit of input.

Example: Response of yield to the seed rate of maize (Hypothetical data)

Sr. No.	Input used (seed rate Kg/ha) 'X'	Total Product (q/ha) Y	Additional input ΔX	Additional Output ΔY	The ratio of Additional Output to additional input i.e. MP= $\Delta Y/\Delta X$
1.	1	10			
2.	2	15			
3.	3	20			
4.	4	25			
5.	5	30			
6.	6	35			

(Draw the graph of the relationship)

From the data, it is seen that for every increase in input unit (1 Kg.), there is an equal or constant increase in the level of output (5 q.) i.e. Marginal product (MP) increases at a constant rate per unit of input.

Hence, this relationship is called as law of constant returns. This input-output relationship gives the total product curve which is a straight line (Linear curve) as shown in the graph. The slope of the curve is constant.

(The relationship can also be expressed as)

$$\frac{\Delta Y_1}{\Delta X_1} = \frac{\Delta Y_2}{\Delta X_2} = \frac{\Delta Y_3}{\Delta X_3} = \frac{\Delta Y_{n-1}}{\Delta X_{n-1}} = \frac{\Delta Y_n}{\Delta X_n}$$

The law of constant returns is not very common in agriculture and it holds only within a limited range

B) Law of increasing returns

The increasing returns to a single factor exist when every additional or marginal unit of input adds more to the total product at an increasing rate per unit of input.

Example: Response of maize yields to the seed rate (Hypothetical data).

Sr. No.	Input used (seed rate Kg/ha) X	Total Product (q/ha) Y	Additional input ΔX	Additional Output ΔY	The ratio of Additional Output to additional input i.e. MP= $\Delta Y/\Delta X$
1.	1	12			
2.	2	14			
3.	3	18			
4.	4	25			
5.	5	29			
6.	6	34			

(Draw the graph of the relationship)

From the table, it is seen that, for every 1 Kg. increase in seed input used, there is an increase in the total output at an increasing rate i.e. marginal product (MP) increases at an increasing rate per unit of input. This input-output relationship gives the total product curve which is convex to the 'X' axis as shown in the graph. The slope of the curve becomes steeper and steeper with the use of additional units of input.

(The relationship can also be expressed as).

$$\frac{\Delta Y_1}{\Delta X_1} < \frac{\Delta Y_2}{\Delta X_2} < \frac{\Delta Y_3}{\Delta X_3} < \frac{\Delta Y_{n-1}}{\Delta X_{n-1}} < \frac{\Delta Y_n}{\Delta X_n}$$

The law of increasing returns exists in agricultural production during the initial stage for only over a short period, observed in a very limited range. This type of return is possible when the fixed factors of production are in excess capacity and the addition of the small unit of various resources makes more and more efficient use of fixed resources.

C) Law of decreasing returns

Here each additional unit of input adds less to the total product (TP) than the previous unit of input. T. P. increases at a decreasing rate per unit of input.

Example: Response of maize yield to the seed rate (Hypothetical data).

Sr. No.	Input used (seed rate Kg/ha) X	Total Product (q/ha) Y	Additional input ΔX	Additional Output ΔY	The ratio of Additional Output to additional input i.e. MP= $\Delta Y/\Delta X$
1.	1	16			
2.	2	26			
3.	3	34			
4.	4	40			
5.	5	44			
6.	6	47			

(Draw the graph of the relationship)

The above example shows decreasing marginal productivity, where the first unit of 1 kg. seed produces 16 q. of output, second 10 q., third 8 q., fourth 6 q., fourth 4 q. and sixth 3 q.

The input-output relationship gives a curve that is not a straight line because the total product increases at a diminishing rate. The shape of the curve is concave to the 'X' axis.

(The relationship can be expressed as)

$$\frac{\Delta Y_1}{\Delta X_1} > \frac{\Delta Y_2}{\Delta X_2} > \frac{\Delta Y_3}{\Delta X_3} > \frac{\Delta Y_{n-1}}{\Delta X_{n-1}} > \frac{\Delta Y_n}{\Delta X_n}$$

This is a technological law of biological response and is applicable in agricultural production under varied farm situations. This law exists in almost all practical situations in agriculture where the addition to the total product decreases with an increase in input. Response to fertilizers, insecticides, seeds, irrigation, feeds, etc. all show diminishing returns.

This law was first put forth by "**Alfred Marshall**"; "as an increase in labour and capital applied to the cultivation of land causes, in general, a less than proportionate increase in the amount of produce unless it happens to coincide with improvements in the art of agriculture".

In simple meaning, it is stated as "if increasing quantities of one input are added to the production process while the quantity of all other inputs is held constant, the quantity of output added per unit of variable input will eventually start declining".

BASIC CONCEPTS

Total Product (TP)

The total amount of output that a firm produces within a given period, which results from the use of different quantities of inputs is called total product (Y)

Marginal product (MP)

The marginal product refers to the change in the output that an additional unit of input factor adds to the total output. It is the ratio of change in total product at a given point to the quantity of input changed.

$$\text{M.P. Per unit of variable input} = \frac{\text{Additional product}}{\text{Additional input}}$$

$$\text{Symbolically it is expressed as MP} = \frac{\Delta Y}{\Delta X}$$

Average Product (AP)

It refers to the average output per unit of the variable input. It is the ratio of the total output to the quantity of input used in producing that amount of output.

$$\text{A. P.} = \frac{\text{Total Output}}{\text{No. of units of inputs used in producing that product}}$$

$$\text{AP} = \frac{Y}{X}$$

Exercise No. 3
TO DETERMINE OPTIMUM INPUT AND OUTPUT COMBINATION AND LEAST COST COMBINATION OF INPUTS

The law of diminishing returns determines the most lucrative level of production as well as the amount of variable input. It is possible to arrange a successful farming business using this straightforward yet effective concept. According to the theory, the amount of output added per unit of variable input will eventually start dropping if greater amounts of one variable input are added to the crop or animal production process after a certain point has been reached, while all other elements remain constant. The level at which one should push the yield per ha. Milk per cow, marketing weight per animal or poultry bird, etc. revolves around the law of diminishing returns. It answers the problem of how much to produce. The added quantity of a variable resource applied to a fixed factor such as land or a given head of livestock adds less and less to the yield or output. Examples are the application of seed, fertilizers, or irrigation to a hectare of land or feeding concentrates and fodder to animals. Some farmers fail to recognize the decreasing returns associated with variable factors, believing that the highest yield per hectare, the highest yield per cow, etc., is always the best option in terms of gross profit. In this sense, they avoid considering costs and returns and instead solely consider physical yield. However, they have to take costs into account at the same time as output. As long as the added return ($MR \geq MC$) is greater than or equal to the additional cost, the profit rule states that the variable resource should be added to the fixed resource indefinitely.

Example

To optimize his earnings, a farmer wants to know how much fertilizer should be applied to one hectare of Jowar. Jowar costs Rs. 800/-per quintal, whereas fertilizer (N) costs Rs. 20/-per kilogram.

Sr. No.	N Kg/ha (X)	Yield q/ha (Y)	Total cost (TC)	Total revenue (TR)	Marginal cost (MC)	Marginal return (MR)	Profit (TR-TC)
1	0	10.0					
2	20	12.0					
3	40	15.0					
4	60	20.0					
5	80	22.0					

7

6	100	23.0					
7	120	23.5					
8	140	23.0					
9	160	22.0					
10	180	21.0					

In the above table compare the marginal or added costs and added return. A farmer should stop applying additional doses of nitrogen where fertilizer cost is just balanced by the added returns from Jowar. Thus, the optimum level of fertilizer in this case is ___________ kg/ha where the profit is maximum i.e. Rs. _______________. Beyond this level, marginal return is less than marginal cost, and profit is declining.

Effect of change in prices

The effect of change in the price of inputs and output also affects the optimum level of input use.

1) Effect of change in price of input

i) Price of Jowar is Rs. 800/- quintal

ii) Price of N – Rs. 8/- per kg. and Rs. 20/- per kg.

N g/ha X	Yield q/ha Y	Additional input ΔX	Additional output ΔY	Added cost at different input prices		Added returns (MR)
				Rs. 8/-	Rs. 20/-	
0	10.0					
20	12.0					
40	15.0					
60	20.0					
80	22.0					
100	23.0					
120	23.5					
140	23.0					
160	22.0					
180	21.0					

When the price of Jowar remains constant at Rs. 800/- q. and the price of N is Rs. 8/- per kg., then _______________ kg. dose of N is most profitable but, when the price of N increase to Rs. 20/- per kg., the ___________ kg. dose of N becomes less profitable, therefore when prices of input are lower, higher doses are most profitable, but when prices of input increase, higher doses are not profitable, and lower doses are profitable.

2) Effect of change in price of output

i) The price of jowar is Rs. 150/q and Rs. 200/q.

ii) Price of N=Rs. 5.50/- per kg.

N kg/ha X	Yield q/ha Y	Additional input ΔX	Additional output ΔY	Additional cost (MC)	Added returns at different output prices			
					Rs.	/-	Rs.	/-
0	10.0							
20	12.0							
40	15.0							
60	20.0							
80	22.0							
100	23.0							
120	23.5							
140	23.0							
160	22.0							
180	21.0							

When the price of nitrogen remains constant at Rs. 5.50/- per kg., and the price of Jowar is Rs. …………./ q., the _______________ kg of N is most profitable. But when the price of Jowar increases to Rs. ________ / q., then ____________ kg of N becomes most profitable. Therefore, when the price of input remains constant or unchanged and the price of output is low, lower doses are more profitable than higher doses, and when the price increase higher doses become more profitable.

Thus, when the output price increase or the input price decrease the optimum level of input increases. Conversely, if the output price decreases or the input price increases the optimum level of input decreases.

To summarize, a farmer can increase the dose of variable input so long as the added returns are greater than the added costs and stop at a point where the added returns are equal to added costs, i.e. MR=MC. That is the maximum profit level or optimum level of input used is directly related to output price and inversely related to input price. Such simple exercises for making day-to-day operational decisions can save the farmer from excessive use of inputs and increase his net returns from the farm business.

This principle should help make decisions of the following type.

1. The level of yield per acre, should be pushed to secure maximum profit (i.e. how much to produce)

2. The size of farm one should operate with given resources of capital, labour, and management

3. The amount of fertilizers, labour, or type of machinery one should use and such other decisions.

Exercise No. 4
TO STUDY LAW OF SUBSTITUTION OR PRINCIPLE OF LEAST COST COMBINATION OF TWO INPUTS

The principle of substitution between two inputs states that if the quantity of output is constant, it is economical to substitute one factor of production for another factor of production if the price of the first input factor is less than the price of the second input factor. This principle provides the logic for determining the least cost method of production. In agricultural Production, it is possible to substitute one input factor for another because argil. Production is dependent on several factors. e.g. farmers may face the problem of deciding whether to prepare seed beds with a wooden plough or iron plough or whether to apply chemical fertilizer or organic manures to produce a given output of crops. In each case, a farmer is interested in selecting the **least-cost practice** or **least-cost combination of resources** for producing a given quantity of produce. Many practices or input factors can be used by the farmer, which allows a large number of combinations of two practices or input factors to produce the desired output. Another example is that, in feeding dairy cows, the farmer can feed a large quantity of Berseem and a small quantity of Concentrates or vice–versa to maintain a given production level of milk. In such a situation a farmer should select such a unique combination so that the cost of two inputs combination is minimum.

To find out the Least Cost Combination of Berseem and Concentrates following steps are necessary.

1. Calculate the added quantity of Berseem and replaced quantity Concentrate taking into consideration the units of two successive levels.

2. Compute the Marginal Rate of Substitution (MRS) by dividing the number of units of replaced resources (i.e. Concentrate) by the number of units of added resource (i.e. Berseem) by using the following formula.

$$\text{MRS} = \frac{\Delta X2}{\Delta X1} = \frac{\text{No. of units of replaced resource}}{\text{No. of units of added resource}}$$

3. Calculate the price ratio (PR) as follows

$$\text{Price Ratio} = \frac{\text{Cost per unit of added resource } (X_1)}{\text{Cost per unit of replaced resource } (X_2)}$$

$$\text{PR} = \frac{P_{X1}}{P_{X2}}$$

1. Work out the Least Cost Combination by equating MRS with price ratio (inverse)

11

$$\frac{\text{Least Cost}}{\text{Combination}} = \frac{\Delta X2}{\Delta X1} = \frac{PX1}{PX2}$$

Example: In the following table different combinations of Berseem (X_1) and Concentrate (X_2) producing 1000 liters of milk have been given. If the price of Berseem is Rs. 10/- per quintal and Concentrate is Rs. 100/- per quintal, work out the Least Cost Combination of Berseem and Concentrate.

Sr. No.	Feed Required to produce 2800 Lit. of Milk		$\Delta X1$	$\Delta X2$	MRS $\dfrac{\Delta X2}{\Delta X1}$	Price Ratio PR = $\dfrac{PX1}{PX2}$
	Berseem (kg) (X_1)	Concentrate (Kg) (X_2)				
1.	7500	900				
2.	7700	850				
3.	7920	800				
4.	8170	750				
5.	8460	700				
6.	8880	650				
7.	9200	600				
8.	9670	550				
9.	10220	500				
10.	10860	450				
11.	11600	400				

Conclusions / Remarks:

NOTE:

1. If MRS is greater than PR go on using more added resources to achieve the Least Cost Combination

$$\frac{\Delta x2}{\Delta x1} > \frac{Px1}{Px2} \qquad \text{Use more quantity of adder resource}$$

2. If MRS is less than PR go on using more of the replaced resources to achieve the Least Cost Combination

$$\frac{\Delta x2}{\Delta x1} < \frac{Px1}{Px2} \qquad \text{Use more quantity of replaced resource}$$

3. When MRS is equal to PR, it is the point where the cost of the combination of two inputs is at the lowest

$$\frac{\Delta x2}{\Delta x1} = \frac{Px1}{Px2}$$

It is the Least Cost Combination

Exercise No. 5
TO DETERMINE THE PROFITABLE COMBINATIONS OF PRODUCTS AND APPLICATION OF THE PRINCIPLE OF EQUI-MARGINAL RETURNS

The principle of diminishing returns helps in determining the most profitable level of resources used under conditions, when resources are available in (indefinite) unlimited quantities, the theory of diminishing returns aids in figuring out the most lucrative degree of resource utilization. The majority of farmers have limited money. Their capital, irrigation capacity, and land are all restricted. During the busiest times for planting and harvesting, even labor—which is regarded as surplus—becomes scarce. The primary goal of a farmer in setting up farm operations is to maximize revenue or profit from each unit of finite resource among the available alternatives when all crops compete for their availability.

The "Principle of Equi-marginal Returns or the Opportunity Cost Principle" is the economic theory that holds in certain situations. It states that the best way to maximize returns from scarce resources is to use them all, adding the most to marginal returns rather than merely maximizing average returns. Every acre of land, every day that labourers and bullocks put in, every kilogram of fertilizer, and every cubic centimeter of water must be used by the farmer in those ventures where they maximize net profits. According to the idea, resources need to be allocated to areas that yield the highest marginal returns rather than the highest average returns.

Example: During the Kharif season, a farmer owns three one-hectare plots where he grows three different varieties of maize. The soil type and natural fertility level of the plots are nearly identical. The following table provides the amount and yield of nitrogen applied.

Nitrogen Per ha X	Added 'N' ΔX	Yield per hectare (Kg.)					
		Jawahar Makka 8		Jawahar Makka 12		Jawahar Makka 216	
		Total	Added	Total	Added	Total	Added
0	--	5870	--	4322	--	4331	--
20		6189		4708		4517	
40		6471		5018		4663	
60		6716		5249		4739	
80		6922		5402		4739	
100		7092		5476		4624	

14

120		7223		5473		4612	
140		7317		5392		4451	
160		7376		5232		4231	
180		7394		4994		3951	
200		7295		4679		3612	

Considering the price of nitrogen Rs. 10/kg. and the price of maize Rs. 6/kg. Calculate the most profitable levels of nitrogen application for each variety.

Complete the table by working out added costs and added returns or marginal returns.

Added N kg/ha	Added cost or marginal cost (Rs.)	Value of added yield of maize or marginal returns (Rs.)		
		Jawahar Makka 8	Jawahar Makka 12	Jawahar Makka 216
20				
20				
20				
20				
20				
20				
20				
20				
20				
20				
Total				
Returns per Kg of Nitrogen				

The most profitable levels for each variety

Jawahar Makka 8	=	Kg. of Nitrogen
Jawahar Makka 12	=	Kg. of Nitrogen
Jawahar Makka 216	=	Kg. of Nitrogen
Total	=	Kg. of Nitrogen

Thus, a farmer needs ________________ kg. of nitrogen to apply for all the varieties at their most profitable level. However, the capital available to him provides to purchase only 200 kg. of nitrogen (Rs. 2000/-). How should he allocate this limited quantity of nitrogen (200 kg.) among the three varieties to get maximum net returns?

Allocation of each does of the limited quantity of nitrogen (i.e. 200 kg.) on different varieties of paddy at a level, which is giving maximum marginal returns.

Dose of Nitrogen (each of 20 kg.)	Variety	Additional income or marginal returns
Ist		
IInd		
IIIrd		
IV th		
Vth		
VIth		
VIIt		
VIII		
IXth		
X th		

The allocation of nitrogen among the three varieties should be as follows

Variety of Maize	Quantity of Nitrogen (Kg)	Additional returns
Jawahar Makka 8		
Jawahar Makka 12		
Jawahar Makka 216		
Total Profit		

It is seen in the above example that, added returns guide the farmer in the allocation of limited resources and not the average returns per kg. of nitrogen. If the farmer considers average returns per kg. of nitrogen, he has to allocate a whole quantity of nitrogen to ________________ variety, because this variety gives the highest increase in income over the two varieties.

This principle is also called the **"Opportunity Cost Principle"** because it considers the value of one enterprise sacrificed as a cost in the production of another enterprise. In this example, the income that the farmer will derive from the _______________ variety and _________________ variety has to sacrifice if he decides to apply all or part of his limited nitrogen to _________________ variety alone, can be considered as the opportunity cost. The cost of nitrogen to Jawahar Makka 8 alone includes the direct cost of nitrogen plus the value of produce from Jawahar Makka 12, and Jawahar Makka 216 which would have to be sacrificed by not applying nitrogen to these varieties.

Now, if the total value of produce from Jawahar Makka 8 exceeds the direct and opportunity cost of nitrogen, it will pay to apply all the nitrogen to Jawahar Makka 8, otherwise, it will be profitable to use nitrogen for Jawahar Makka 12, and Jawahar Makka 216 variety.

The opportunity cost of an input to a farmer is the value in its best alternative use. If a bullock pair earns Rs. 100/day on ploughing, but can also earn Rs. 150/- per day in the employment, say carting in Kharif season. In this case, if the farmer carries out a ploughing operation first, considering the urgency of farm operations, then the opportunity cost of using a resource (bullock pair) will be Rs. 150/- for ploughing.

Practical Utility of the Concept to the Farmer

1. It guides the farmer to plan his budget for the preparation of his cropping scheme and fitting therein his livestock program.

2. It enables him to determine enterprise is combination-complementary or competitive in the budgeting of the farm.

3. It guides the adoption of diversified or specialized farming, as there is a profitable limit for each enterprise as well as the most profitable enterprise for each farm.

TO STUDY VARIOUS DEPRECIATION METHOD

Depreciation refers to the amount of value that a farm asset loses due to factors other than a shift in the item's overall cost is known as depreciation. Stated differently, it can be characterized as the decline of an asset's value due to usage, deterioration, mishaps, and eventual obsolescence. (i.e. becoming out of date due to a new invention). The decline in value is gradual and takes place through wear and tear of implements, use of buildings, aging of animals, etc. Thus, depreciation involves the distribution of the original value or cost of an asset over its useful life. The amount of depreciation charges should match the asset's gradual decline in value. If every item bought was worn out by the end of the year, depreciation would not need to be calculated. Nonetheless, over an extended period, assets like buildings, machinery, cattle, etc. steadily deplete, raising significant questions on how to determine their initial value. The asset may lose all of its value or only have its garbage value left.

Points to be considered in Computing Depreciation

1. Original value i.e. construction cost or purchase price

2. Estimated useful life in years

3. Value at the end of useful life (i.e. junk value scrap value residual value or salvage value).

4. Changes of obsolescence

Methods of Computing Depreciation

There are many methods of computation of depreciation, but none of these methods can be considered the most appropriate under all circumstances. The methods of computing depreciation can be based on either of the following two assumptions.

1. Assets are used at a constant rate year after year, and

2. Assets are used at varying rates year after year.

The Methods of Depreciation Computation

1. Straight line method

2. Diminishing balance or value method

3. Sum of the year digits or Reducing fraction method

4. Compound interest method

5. Annual revaluation method

6. Machine hour basis method

1. Straight Line Method

This is the most commonly used method. It is easy, simple, and usually very satisfactory for most purposes. This method assumes that assets are used more or less to the same extent every year and therefore, an equal amount of costs on account of their use can be charged every year. This method consists of dividing the total anticipated depreciation by the number of years the particular asset is expected to lose. The total anticipated depreciation is the purchase price of the article minus junk value/salvage value/scrap value/residual value. By this method, the amount of annual deprecation will be calculated by using the following formula

$$\text{Amount of annual depreciation} = \frac{\text{Original price of the asset} - \text{junk value}}{\text{No. of useful years of asset (expected life)}}$$

In this method, the fixed percentage on the original value of the asset is charged annually to reduce it to junk value at the end of the estimated useful life. This annual charge of a fixed amount is deducted from the value of an asset, at the end of each year

Example 1:   Calculate the value of a bullock cart at the end of the 5ᵗʰ year with the help of data given below

1. Original value of the Bullock cart Rs. 20000/-

2. Useful   life   of 10 years

3. Junk value   Rs. 2000/-

Solution

Amount of annual depreciation

= Original price – Annual depreciation ÷ Years used

=

Example 2: Calculate the value of a farm store in 2023 based on the following data

1. Original cost   =   Rs. 50000/-

2. Year of construction   =   2000

3. Junk value   =   10 % of the construction cost

4. Annual rate of depreciation $\qquad$ = $\qquad$ 2 %

Solution

1. Annual rate of depreciation $\qquad$ =

2. Annul amount of depreciation $\qquad$ =

3. Value of farm store in the year 2023 =

2. Diminishing balance or value method

In this method, a fixed rate of depreciation is used for every year and applied to the value of the asset at the beginning of the year. The original cost or value of an asset is divided by its estimated life to know the fixed percentage. This fixed rate is applied to the balance amount up to the salvage value is reached and no further depreciation is possible. Under this method, the amount of depreciation is higher in the earlier life of the article and lower in later years.

Illustration

A machine is purchased for Rs. 1000/- and its expected life is 10 years. Calculated the depreciated value of the machine at the end of each year.

Solution

Given:

1) Original value/purchase cost $\qquad$ = $\qquad$ Rs. 10000/-

2) Expected life $\qquad$ = $\qquad$ 10 years

3) Annual depreciation rate $\qquad$ = $\dfrac{\text{Rs. 10000/-}}{\text{Expected life}}$

i.e. Rs. 1000/-

Rs. 1000/- is 10% of the original value (10000/-). Therefore, the rate of a fixed percentage of annual depreciation will be 10%.

With the help of the given information calculate depreciation and residual values for each year.

(Values in Rs.)

Year	Value at the beginning of the year	Amount of annual depreciation	Diminishing or Residual value at the end of the year
1	10000/-	1000/-	(10000 – 1000) = 9000
2	1000/-	900/-	(9000-900) = 8100
3			

4			
5			
6			
7			
8			
9			
10			

3. Sum of the year digits or reducing fraction method

By this method, the annual depreciation is calculated by multiplying a fraction times the amount to be depreciated (i.e. original value minus scrap value). The fraction for any year can be determined by the following formula

$$\text{Fraction for any year} = \frac{\text{The year of life remaining at the beginning of the accounting year}}{\text{The sum of the years of life of the asset}}$$

$$\text{Fraction for 1}^{\text{st}}\text{ year} = \frac{10}{1+2+3+4+5+6+7+8+9+10} = \frac{10}{55}$$

$$\text{Fraction for 2}^{\text{nd}}\text{ year} = \frac{9}{1+2+3+4+5+6+7+8+9+10} = \frac{9}{55}$$

Thus, the sum of the year digits in the case of an asset having an expected life of ten years is 55. The total amount of depreciation (original value – scrap value) for the entire life of the asset is to be divided by 55 units. For the 1st year, the depreciation charges would be 10/55 of the total depreciation, for the second year 9/55, and so on.

Example: Calculate the value at the end of each year of an asset purchased at Rs. 12000/- with a salvage value of Rs. 1000/- and an expected life of 10 years.

1. Sum of the year digits = (1+2+3 ……………………… + 10 = 55 units)

2. Total amount of deprecation = 12000 – 1000 = Rs. 11000/-

Year	Value at the beginning of the year (Rs.)	Annual depreciation (Rs.)	Value of the end of the year (Rs.)

1	12000/-	11000 × (10/55) = 2000	12000 – 2000 = 10000
2	10000	11000 × (9/55) = 1800	10000 – 1800 = 8200
3			
4			
5			
6			
7			
8			
9			
10			

4. Annual revaluation method

This method involves fixing of values of assets annually. The assets are valued consistently with the market value of the asset at the end of each year. If the revaluation amount is less than the book value of the asset, the difference is depreciation (Loss) and if it is greater, the difference is appreciation (Profit). This method is suitable and applied for calculating depreciation or appreciation of livestock.

The defect of this method is that the amount of depreciation charged every year is in unequal sums though the asset performs the same service year after year.

6. Machine hour basis method

In this method, the rate of depreciation is calculated considering the number of hours a machine runs in a year

$$\text{Depreciation per hour} = \frac{\text{Purchase value} - \text{Scrap value}}{\text{Life of Machine (Hrs.)}}$$

$$\text{Deprecation in a particular year} = \text{Per hour depreciation} \times \text{Use of the machine in a particular year (Hrs.)}$$

Example

A machine costs Rs. 21000/- and is expected to run for 10 years, after which its scrap value will be Rs. 3000/-. The machine is expected to run 1000 hrs./year. Estimate the depreciation charges per hour of the machine.

Solution:

TO STUDY VARIOUS TYPES OF COSTS AND THEIR COMPUTATION METHODS

In farming, the relationship between production costs and income is very crucial. When making manufacturing decisions, producers must examine the cost of production very carefully.

In farming, there are two accounting periods: the short-run period and the long-run period. The short-run period is the time frame within which desirable production adjustments can be made without modifying the farm's size or organizational structure. One crop season or an agricultural year could qualify as such a time frame. Generally speaking, the long run period is the amount of time that is adequate to allow changes in the organization or even the size of the farm to affect the output level.

As there are two time periods, there are two corresponding costs. I) Fixed costs or sunk costs or overhead costs (long-run-cost) II) Variable costs (Short-run-costs).

Fixed Costs

They remain unchanged regardless of output volume. These comprise the farm's overhead costs, which need to be covered even in the event of no production. Examples are land rent and taxes, depreciation, charges of permanent hired labour, maintenance of bullocks, milch animals, and other animals, etc.

Variable Costs

The price of utilizing variable inputs is known as a variable cost. Costs that change depending on the volume of output are known as variable costs. The price of including variable inputs is one of them. If there is no production, they do not happen. For instance, the price of seed, fertilizers, paid labour each day, petrol or energy costs, the cost of feeding milch animals as fodder, etc.

Total Costs

Fixed costs plus variable costs are equal to total costs. Net income is equal to total income (or gross income) minus total costs. A farmer will have to quit farming if total costs are more than total income in the long-run period.

Identification of fixed and variable costs helps in making short-run and long-run decisions.

In the short run, gross income must at least cover variable costs, and maximum net income is obtained when marginal cost (MC) is equal to marginal return (MR). If gross income is less than the total cost (Fixed and Variable costs) but is still greater than the variable costs then the guiding principle is to "go on increasing production so long as MR are greater than MC" so that the loss is minimized. From the point of view regarding day-to-day management decisions variable costs are important.

In the long run, gross income should necessarily be greater than the total costs (fixed and variable costs). For making production decisions in such a situation, one should go on using resources as long as MR is greater than MC. Net returns are maximum when MR=MC, here objective is to maximize profits instead of minimizing the losses. In the long run, there are no fixed costs. All costs become variable costs.

Table 1: Illustration of fixed and variable costs on a one-hectare farm.

Sr. No	Particulars	Level of production (Maize)		
		10q	20q	30q
A)	**Variable costs**	Rs.	Rs.	Rs.
	i) Hired labour charges	400	550	200
	ii) Seeds	200	275	450
	iii) Fertilizers	300	550	750
	iv) Electricity charges	400	650	850
	v) Pesticides	70	110	160
	vi) other expenses	100	160	280
	Total variable costs			
	Average variable costs /Q.			
B)	**Fixed cost**	Rs.	Rs.	Rs.
	i) Land Revenue	110	110	110
	ii) Depreciation on building and equipment	300	500	500
	iii) Interest on fixed capital	650	650	650
	iv) Other fixed costs	150	150	150
	Total fixed costs			
	Average fixed costs /Q.			
C)	**Total cost (Fixed + Variable)**			
	Average total cost /Q.			

Concepts and computation of different costs

To know the relationship between different types of costs we need to know AFC, AVC, ATC, and MC

- **Average Fixed Cost (AFC)**

It is worked out by dividing total fixed costs by the amount of output. It is a fixed cost per unit of output. It varies for each level of output. As output increases, AFC decreases. Thus, per-unit fixed costs are estimated by using the following formula.

$$AFC = \frac{\text{Total fixed costs}}{\text{Amount of output}} = \frac{TFC}{Y}$$

- **Average Variable Cost (AVC)**

It is worked out by dividing total variable cost by the amount of output Average variable cost varies with the level of output. It will decrease in the beginning when the law of increasing returns operates and then increase when the law of diminishing returns operates. It is inversely proportional to the average product i.e. when APP increases AVC decreases and as APP decreases AVC increases.

$$AVC = \frac{\text{Total variable cost}}{\text{Amount of output}} = \frac{TVC}{Y}$$

- **Average Total Cost (ATC)**

It is the total cost per unit of output. It decreases in the beginning when the law of increasing returns operates and then increases when the law of diminishing returns operates.

$$ATC = \frac{\text{Total cost}}{\text{Amount of output}} = \frac{TC}{Y}$$

OR

$$ATC = AFC + AVC$$

- **Marginal Cost (MC)**

The marginal cost or added cost is the cost incurred for producing an additional unit of output. In other words, the cost of producing an additional unit of output. It is computed by dividing the change in total cost (ΔTC) by the corresponding change in output (ΔY) i.e.

$$MC = \frac{\Delta TC}{\Delta Y}.$$

Relationship of Costs

1. As the output increases, the average fixed cost (AFC) goes on declining continuously, because the fixed cost is constant while the output (denominator) increases.

2. The average variable cost (AVC) first declines so long as the law of increasing returns holds good but after a certain point is reached, it starts increasing because of the operation of the law of diminishing returns.

3. The average total cost (ATC) first declines, reaches a minimum, and then increases, (the ATC curve is at a higher level of output than that of the AVC curve)

4. The marginal cost (MC) which is defined as the change in total cost divided by the change in output ($\Delta TC / \Delta Y$) declines first, reaches a minimum, and then starts increasing.

5. So long as the AVC is declining, the MC is less than the AVC, when the AVC starts increasing MC becomes greater than the AVC. Naturally, when the AVC is minimum, it is equal to MC i.e. MC curve cuts AVC from below at its minimum.

6. The MC curve starts from below the AVC curve and cuts AVC curves at its minimum or lowest point and afterward goes higher than AVC and ATC respectively.

The decision for profit maximization

Go on increasing the production as long as the marginal costs (MC) are less than or equal to marginal returns (MR) so that the profit is maximum. As soon as the MC exceeds MR, the profit starts declining. One should stop production, where MC=MR.

Example:

The data regarding output, returns, and cost is given in Table 2. Using this data estimate the different costs and complete the table. Also, draw a graph of cost function (Different costs) and study their relationship.

Table 2: Relationship between different types of costs and returns

Output Qtl/ha. (Y)	Total returns (@Rs. 100/q.) (Rs.)	Fixed costs FC (Rs.)	Variable cost VC (Rs.)	Total cost TC (FC+VC) (Rs.)	Average fixed cost AFC (FC/Y) (Rs.)	Average variable cost AVC (VC/Y) (Rs.)	Average total cost ATC (TC/Y) (Rs.)	Marginal cost $\Delta TC/\Delta Y$ (Rs.)	Marginal returns	Profit (TR-TC) (Rs.)
10	1000	1250	420							
20	2000	1250	640							
30	3000	1250	720							

40	4000	1250	9040							
50	5000	1250	1700							
60	6000	1250	2570							
70	7000	1250	3730							

Exercise No. 8
TO STUDY PREPARATION OF FARM PLANS

Planning is the deliberate and conscious effort on the part of the farmer to think about the farm programmers in advance and adjust them according to new knowledge on technological developments, changes in physical and economic situations, price structures, etc.

Scientific planning is situations written based on the best information available and aimed at achieving the maximum satisfaction for the farmer and his family out of their resources.

What is Farm Planning?

Farm planning implies the adoption of business methods in every phase of farm activity. It is a decision-making process. The farm planning approach is an integrated, co-ordinate and advanced Programme of actions, which seeks to present an opportunity for cultivators to improve their level of income

Farm planning is an approach that introduces desirable changes in farm organization and operations and makes the farm a viable unit. Farm planning is a process of making decisions regarding the organization and operation of a farm business so that it results in a continuous maximization of the net returns of a farm business.

Why Farm Planning?

On the majority of our farms, there is under-utilization as well as overutilization of the existing farm resources. Due to this, our farmers fail to get optimum and maximum net gains. There is an immediate necessity to reorganize the farm structure and for the proper allocation of resources to obtain maximum net income and optimum production. This calls for proper farm planning and budgeting.

The main objective of farm planning is to maximize net income and it involves "Planning Horizon". The length of the planning period based on the farmer's situation has to be therefore decided. The main objective is to maximize the annual net income sustained over a long period.

Types of Farm Planning

1) **Simple farm planning** is adopted either for a part of the land, for one enterprise, or to substitute one resource for another. This is very simple and easy to understand as well as to implement. The process of change should always begin with simple farm planning.

2) **Complete farm planning** envisages farm planning for the whole farm, i.e. for all enterprises on the farm, for a change in the farm structure and organization. Complete farm planning aims for a complete change in the cropping Programme, more towards specialized farming, more income, and market orientation.

Essential Elements of Farm Planning

Economic planning involves the manipulation of limited resources among alternative opportunities, to satisfy the set objective of maximizing profit. It follows that any planning procedure must contain three essential elements:

(1) an objective, (2) scarce resources, and (3) the enterprise for using the resources to attain the objective (alternative ways).

The main aim or objective in planning the allocation of resources is to maximize profit. However, farmers commonly have other objectives as well, which must be taken into account in practical planning. In any form of planning, the principle of profit maximization cannot be abandoned. The resources available to the farmer act as a framework, within which he must plan his farm activities. The concern is with those resources that are relatively scarce. Although it is frequently impossible to decide in advance which resources will prove to be limiting, so that is becomes part of the planning process, to detect them. The resources available to the farmer distinguish the feasible from the unfeasible enterprises. Fixed resources place a limit on the maximum level of production; from individual enterprises fixed resources influence the level of input, both of other fixed resources and variable resources. The limitations of resources determine the most suitable organization to be added within individual enterprises.

The enterprises are the third element, representing alternative ways of using fixed resources in seeking to attain the objective. The information that is required about the enterprises before planning are:

1) Financial returns

2) Requirements of variable inputs

3) Requirements of fixed resources

Without information on the financial return to be expected in the enterprises, it would be impossible to attain the set objective of maximizing net income because there would be no criterion on which to base their selection. Variable inputs are items such as fertilizers, feed stuffs, etc., the use of which alters in direct proportion to changes in the balance of individual enterprises, within a given framework of fixed resources. Many factors affect the level of variable inputs. They include the quality of fixed resources, the intensity of production, the methods adopted, and the efficiency with which they are applied. The financial returns and the variable costs have one feature in common, namely they both vary together with changes in the size of enterprises. Deducting the variable costs from the output of an enterprise leaves the gross margin and it is the latter that becomes the guide, as to which enterprises to select in seeking to maximize net income. The fixed resources available at any particular point in time constitute a planning framework; the unit requirements of fixed resources vary with the production methods adopted and the relative efficiency with which they are applied. It is possible to raise the limits imposed on an enterprise, both by lowering fixed resource requirements and by acquiring more fixed resources. Knowledge of fixed resource requirements is also needed to enable the return (gross margin) to the resources used in different enterprises to be calculated.

Stages of Farm Planning

Stage 1: Adoption of a package of practices (selected enterprises) – envisages no change in the cropping pattern.

Stage 2: Extension of stage 1 to all crop enterprises on the farm. Here also no major change is envisaged. The farmer has to use all the recommended practices on all the major enterprises simultaneously.

Stage 3: Final stage full farm plan. The major change is envisaged in farm structure and organization. It requires considerable training in farm management. Detailed farm plans are to be prepared to get maximum income from resources.

Principal Characteristics of a Good Farm Plan

1) It should provide for efficient use of farm resources, such as labour, power, and equipment.

2) The crop plan should have a balanced combination of enterprises, i.e. it should do the following:

   a) Provide for given minimum production of different food, cash and fodder crops.

   b) Help to maintain and improve soil fertility.

   c) Help to raise and stabilize farm earnings

   d) Improve distribution and use of labour, power and water requirements throughout the year

   e) Avoid excessive risks

f) Provide flexibility

g) Utilize, the farmers knowledge, training, experience and take into account of the farmers likes and dislikes

h) Give considerations to efficient marketing facilities

i) Provide Programme of obtaining, using and repaying the credit

j) Provide for all of up-to date modern agricultural methods and practices.

Basic Steps of Farm Planning and Budgeting

1) Assessment of resources- survey of actual conditions of the farm and the availability or resources and use

2) Analysis of the existing plan operations

3) Identification the problems, detection of loop-holes and defects of the present plans.

4) Discussion with the farmers and other specialists to examine the possibilities for improvement through alternative plan operations

5) Preparation of alternative plans on the basis of existing co-efficient and discussion with the farmer

6) Selection of final plan for implementation.

TO STUDY PREPARATION AND ANALYSIS OF THE BALANCE SHEETS FOR FARMS

Every farmer, regardless of size, tracks the farm's financial performance over some time or during an agricultural year. The possibility exists that the various groups of farmers will exhibit varying degrees of keenness. Put another way, when a farm grows in size, the capital needed to operate it also grows, necessitating greater caution on the part of the farmer to manage the farm because there is a greater danger of any unanticipated event. When it comes to controlling larger financial outlays, the management component is essential. However, in the farming sector, financial management is just as crucial for small farmers, if not more so than for large farmers. The farm business's financial soundness is shown by the balance sheet, which provides an account of all assets and all liabilities. More precisely, it is an asset, liability, and equity statement that represents the financial standing of a farm business at a certain point in time. Net worth, also referred to as equity, is the amount of assets less the amount of obligations; net deficit is the opposite. The typical balance sheet (Table 1) shows assets on the left side and liabilities and equity on the right side. Both sides are always in balance hence the name balance sheet. Net worth is placed on the right side, along with liabilities, to indicate that like any other creditor, the farmer has a claim against the farm business equal to the equity amount. The balance sheet can be easily prepared by the farmer in the presence of farm records. It can be prepared at any point in time to know the financial position of the farm business. It can also be prepared to study the performance of a business over the years by preparing the same number of balance sheets. If the net worth increases over the different periods, it indicates the efficient performance of the business. To prepare a balance sheet the prime requisites are total assets and total liabilities of the farm.

- **Assets:** Assets are those which are owned by the farmer.

  Assets are of three types, viz. current, intermediate or working, and long-term or fixed. So as the liabilities. This classification of assets facilitates the analysis of the liquidity of the farm business.

  Current assets: They are very liquid or short-term assets. They can be converted into cash, within a short time, usually one year. For example, cash on hand, agricultural produce ready for disposal, i.e., stocks of paddy, black gram, Jowar, wheat, etc.

Intermediate or working assets: These assets take two to five years to convert into cash form. Examples: Machinery, equipment, livestock, tractors, trucks, etc.

- **Liabilities:** These refer to all things that are owed to others by the farmer.

- **Long-term assets or fixed assets:** An asset that is permanent or will be used continuously for several years is called a long-term asset. It takes a longer time to convert into cash due to the verification of records, legal transactions, etc. Examples: Land, Farm buildings, etc.

- **Current liabilities:** Debts that must be paid in the short term or very soon. Examples: Crop loans, other loans, cost of maintenance of cattle, etc.

- **Intermediate liabilities:** These loans are due for repayment within a period of two to five years. Examples: livestock loans, machinery loans, etc.

- **Long-term liabilities:** The duration of loan repayment is five or more years. Examples: Tractor loan, orchard loan, land development loan, etc.

Table 1. Balance Sheet of a Hypothetical Farm

Assets	Amount (in Rs)	Liabilities	Amount (in Rs)
Current assets		**Current liabilities**	
Cash on hand	10,000	Crop loans to be repaid to institutional agencies	8,000
Savings in bank	8,000		
Value of grains ready for disposal	38,500	Cost of cultivation (excluding loans)	6,000
Livestock products (eggs, birds, etc.)	60,000	Other loans (unsecured loans due for immediate repayment)	5,000
Fruits, Vegetables, fodder and feed ready for sale	9,000	Cost of maintenance of cattle Costs in poultry enterprise	3,600 25,000
Value of bonds and shares to be realized in the same year	3,000	Annual installments	20,000
Sub-total	**1,28,500**	**Sub-total**	**67,600**
Intermediate assets		**Intermediate liabilities**	
Dairy cattle	10,000	Livestock loans	8,000
Bullocks	9,000	Machinery loan	15,000

Poultry birds	15,000	Unsecured loans	10,000
Tractor	1,76,000		
Sub-total	**2,25,000**	**Sub-total**	**33,000**
Long-term assets		**Long-term liabilities**	
Land (book value)	60,00,000	Tractor loan	1,20,000
Farm buildings	25,000	Orchard loan	25,000
		Unsecured loans	10,000
Sub-total	**6,25,000**	**Sub-total**	**1,55,000**
Total of assets	**9,78,500**	**Total of liabilities**	**2,55,600**
		Net worth or equity	**7,22,900**
		Total of liabilities +net worth	**9,78,500**

Precautions in Preparing the Balance Sheet of a Business Farm (Firm)

(1) Accuracy in the valuation of assets is difficult in the absence of records, hence approximations to such valuations need to be defined concerning a given time. All farm products say, paddy, pulses, oilseeds, jowar, livestock and livestock products, etc., should be valued based on the market price. Land and other non-liquid assets should be valued based on the prevailing sale value for similar types of land at the same time.

(2) While valuing durable assets, the book value method (valuing at cost) is no doubt a good procedure but is subject to criticism. For example, if a farmer bought his farmlands in different periods say, 1960 and 1970, the book value of these lands should be determined after giving an allowance for depreciation and improvements made on the land and

(3) In periods of inflation, the values of durable assets rise. Under such situations, it is desirable to make adjustments in the values of the assets, while entering the same in the balance sheet.

(Note: Book value refers to the realistic value of an asset giving due allowance for depreciation and improvement. Hence, book value is neither the market price nor purchase price, but value at cost.)

Test Ratios

The test ratios, viz. current ratio, intermediate ratio, net capital ratio, quick ratio, current liability ratio, debt-equity ratio, and equity-value ratio can be derived from the balance sheet.

$$1.\ \text{Current ratio} = \frac{\text{Total current assets}}{\text{Total current liabilities}}$$

$$= \frac{1,28,500}{67,600} = 1.90$$

This ratio indicates the capacity of the farmer to meet immediate financial obligations (liquidity). If current assets are more than current liabilities and if the borrower fails to repay the loan, this is a case of willful default despite his position being solvent. This type of willful default is more common in respect of large farmer-borrowers of financial institutions. If by chance the ratio falls less than one due to certain unforeseen contingencies, his case for further lending cannot be ruled out by the institutional agencies, as it is a temporary setback and he may be given a chance to prove his creditworthiness. A ratio of more than one indicates a favorable run of the farm business. The current ratio reflects liquidity within one year.

$$2.\ \text{Intermediate ratio or working ratio} = \frac{\text{Total current assets} + \text{Total intermediate assets}}{\text{Total current liabilities} + \text{Total intermediate liabilities}}$$

$$= \frac{1,28,500 + 2,25,000}{67,600 + 33,000} = \frac{3,53,500}{1,00,600} = 3.51$$

This indicates the liquidity position of the farm business over an intermediate period, ranging from 2 to 5 years. Here certain time is allowed for the farmer to build up the farm business to improve his liquidity position. This ratio should also be more than one to indicate the sound running of the farm business. The progressive intermediate ratio observed for giving farm business over time implies, the increase in the value of current and intermediate assets due to minimal physical loss and price decline. The steady growth of this ratio over a period is a healthy sign of the business.

$$3.\ \text{Net capital ratio} = \frac{\text{Total assets}}{\text{Total liabilities}}$$

$$= \frac{9,78,500}{2,55,600}$$

$$= 3.82$$

It indicates the solvency position of the farmers. If the net capital ratio is more than one, the funds of institutional agencies are safe. A consistently increasing ratio over the years reveals the sound financial growth of the farm business. The farmer with this record should be a very prompt repayer of all types of credit obligations. This ratio is also the most important measure of the overall solvency position of the farmer-borrowers.

4. Acid test ratio or quick ratio =

$$\frac{\text{Cash receipts} + \text{accounts receivable} + \text{marketable securities}}{\text{Total current liabilities}}$$
(bonds, shares, etc.) Available for more than one year

This reflects the adequacy of cash and income surpluses to cover all current liabilities during the period of one to two years. If there is no difference in the income position of a farmer within that period, the current ratio and acid test ratio reflect the same position.

$$5. \text{ Current liability ratio} = \frac{\text{Current Liabilities}}{\text{Owner's equity}}$$

$$\text{Current liability ratio} = \frac{67,600}{7,22,900}$$

$$= 0.09$$

This ratio indicates the farmer's immediate financial obligations against the net worth. A ratio of less than one indicates a healthy performance of the farm business and over the years the ratio should become smaller and smaller to reflect a consistently good performance.

$$6. \text{ Debt-equity ratio (Leverage ratio)} = \frac{\text{Total debts}}{\text{Owner's equity}}$$

$$= \frac{2,55,600}{7,22,900} = 0.35$$

This presents the capacity of the farmer to meet the long-term commitments. Also, it throws light on the extent of indebtedness in the farm business or conversely, the amount of capital raised by the farmer in running the farm business. A consistently falling ratio indicates a very heartening performance of farming and the ability of the farmer to reduce dependence on borrowings.

$$7. \text{ Equity value ratio} = \frac{\text{Owner's equity}}{\text{Value of assets}}$$

$$= \frac{7,22,900}{9,78,500} = 0.73$$

This ratio highlights the productivity gained by the farmer of the assets he has. The improvement in the ratio over the years makes it crystal clear regarding the increased strength in the financial structure of the farm business. This ratio has a direct bearing on the type of assets one has. The managerial competence of the farmer is an essential element in raising the productivity of the assets.

PREPARATION AND ANALYSIS OF PROFIT AND LOSS STATEMENT

Income Statement or Profit and Loss Statement

This is entirely different from a balance sheet in the sense that in a balance sheet, we considered assets and liabilities and did not consider operational efficiency in terms of receipts and expenses. In the income statement, the items included are receipts, expenses, gains, and losses. It could be defined as a summary of receipts and gains minus expenses and losses during a specified period. It is prepared for the entire farm for one agricultural year. In the income statement, monetary values are assigned to inputs and output. It is also prepared over time. The advantages of this statement are that it indicates the trend in various cost items and whether there has been any over-expenditure on the farm. Thus, it helps to know the success or failure of a business farm over time. The income statement constitutes three items. viz., receipts, expenses, and net income. The income statement of a hypothetical farm is presented in Table 2.

- **Receipts:** They mean the returns obtained from the sale of crop produce and other supplementary products like milk and eggs, wages, gifts, etc. Gain in the form of appreciation in the value of assets is also included in the receipts. However, returns from the sale of capital assets, such as livestock, machinery, farm buildings, etc. are not included because such return/income is not obtained during the period.

- **Expenses:** Operating and fixed costs are recorded here. Losses in the form of depreciation on the asset value fall under the expenditure item. However, the amounts incurred on the purchase of capital assets are not considered.

- **Net income:** It constitutes net cash income, net operating income, and net farm income.

- **Net cash income:** It gives the position of cash receipts minus cash expenses only during the period for which the income statement is prepared.

- **Net operating income:** It is arrived at by deducting operating expenses from the gross income. Fixed costs are not given any consideration. Operating expenses include crop loans.

- **Net farm income:** Net farm income equals net operating income less fixed costs. Compared to net cash income and net operating income, it is relatively a better measure of assessing the performance of a farm. It is the return accrued to own capital and family labour employed.

- **Income statement:** It is prepared for a given farm for a given year and may present a very bright picture of the farm. The same position cannot be taken for granted as the actual position of the farm, since the said year might have been a good agricultural year concerning weather, yields, prices, etc. A realistic position on the performance of a farm can be gauged by preparing income statements over years to show the actual situation, as the parameters influencing farm business are subject to fluctuations

Table 2. Income Statement of a Hypothetical Farm

	Particulars	Amount (In Rs.)
I.	**Receipts**	
A.	Returns from the sale of crop output (paddy + pulse)	52,000
B.	Revenue from milk and milk products	5,000
	Return from poultry enterprise	12,000
	Returns from supplementary enterprises	————
		17,000
C.	Gifts	2,000
D.	Gross cash income	71,000
E.	Appreciation of the value of assets	3,000
F.	Gross income	74,000
II	**Expenses (Operating expenses or costs)**	
A.	Hired human labour	10,500
B.	Bullock labour	900
C.	Machine labour	1,500
D.	Seeds	1,100
E.	Feeds	5,000
F.	Manures & fertilizers	3,000
G.	Plant protection measures	1,550
H.	Veterinary aid	500
I.	Irrigation	250
J.	Miscellaneous	2,000
K.	Interest on working capital	2,100
	Total operating expenses	28,400

III.	**Fixed expenses or costs**	
A.	Depreciation	3,000
B.	Land revenue	200
C.	Interest on fixed capital (includes interest of Rs 1500 paid towards term loan)	3,200
D.	Rental value of owned land	10,000
E.	Total fixed costs	16,400
IV.	**Net cash income**	71,000 – 28,400 = 42,600
V.	**Net operating income**	74,000 – 28,400 = 45,600
VI.	**Net farm income**	45,600 – 16,400 = 29,200

Farm Income and Profit Efficiency Measures

Financial Test Ratios

The performance of the farm business as indicated in Table 1, can be assessed through the income analysis by gainfully using two important parameters, viz. costs and returns. Still, some additional information is left untouched if we do not regard financial test ratios, as they supplement new information. These help the farmers themselves as well as lending institutions, and help in developing standard norms. Two sets of income ratios can be developed. One is directly from the income and expenditure pattern, and another by taking one component from the income statement i.e., income levels, and comparing it against capital investment made on the farm business. The former ratios are called expense-income ratios and the latter, investment-income ratios.

Following are the ratios which can be obtained directly from the income statement.

$$\text{Operating ratio} = \frac{\text{Total operating expenses}}{\text{Gross income}}$$

$$= \frac{28,400}{74,000} = 0.38$$

As the very name reveals, the ratio explains the relationship between operating costs to gross income. This ratio underlines the magnitude of working expenditure incurred for a rupee of gross income. This is a direct ratio which works out to 0.38.

$$\text{Fixed ratio} = \frac{\text{Fixed expenses}}{\text{Gross income}}$$

$$= \frac{16,400}{74,000} = 0.22$$

This ratio indicates the relationship between fixed expenses and gross income. This particular ratio is 0.22. It depicts the amount of fixed expenses incurred to realize a rupee of gross income. This is an indirect ratio since fixed costs are indirect costs.

$$\text{Gross ratio} = \frac{\text{Total expenses}}{\text{Gross income}}$$

$$= \frac{44,800}{74,000} = 0.61$$

This is the ratio that is obtained when both operating expenses and fixed expenses are totaled up and compared with gross income. This can be called the input-output ratio, which amounted to 0.61.

All these ratios should be less than one to indicate the profitable run of the farm business. When these ratios are estimated over some time, a healthy trend of farm business is reflected by the descending ratios.

Investment-Income Ratios: The following two are the ratios that fall under this category.

$$\text{Capital turnover ratio} = \frac{\text{Gross income}}{\text{Average capital investment}}$$

$$= \frac{74,000}{3,00,000} = 0.25$$

This is also a self-explanatory ratio as explained earlier. Here, average capital investment is arrived at by adding the value of assets at the beginning of the agricultural year and the end of the agricultural year and then averaging the two values. Suppose it is Rs. 3,00,000, then the capital turnover ratio is 0.25. This ratio gives the gross income obtained for each rupee of capital invested over the year.

$$\text{Rate of return on investment} = \frac{\text{Net return to capital}}{\text{Average capital investment}}$$

$$= \frac{27,800}{3,00,000} = 0.09$$

Net return to capital is obtained by adding bank interest paid (interest on borrowed funds + interest paid on term loans) to the net farm income and then deducting unpaid family labour for farm and livestock operations and management.

Net farm income (in Rs.)   =   29,200

Interest paid during the year (in Rs.)   = + 3,600

                                                              32,800

Unpaid family labour wages (in Rs.) =   - 5,000

Net return to total capital (in Rs.)   =   27,800

This ratio (0.09) gives the net return on capital for every rupee of average capital invested. These above two ratios relate to the income-generating capacity of the investment and are hence called income-investment ratios.

Exercise No. 11
TO STUDY FARM HOLDING SURVEY

1) Information of cultivator:

i. Name: _____________________________   ii. Age: _______________

iii. Education: _____________________   iv. Village: _______________

v. Occupation:

a) Main: ____

b) Subsidiary ____

vi. Size of the family:

Sr. No.	Age Group	Male	Female	Total
a)	Up to 14 years			
b)	Above 14 years			
c)	Members working on the farm			

2) Operational holding:

Sr. No.	Particulars	Area (ha)	Land revenue and other ceases (Rs.)	Per ha. Value (Rs.)

1.	Cultivated
	    a) Irrigated
	    b) Unirrigated			

2.	Uncultivated			
3.	Barren land			
	Total			

3) Cropping Pattern: (Year: -------------)

Sr. No.	Crops	Variety	Area (ha)	
			Irrigated	Unirrigated

A)	Kharif Season
	    1.
	    2.			

B)	Rabi/ Summer Season
	    1.
	    2.			

C)	Perennial
	    1. Mango
	    2. cashew
	    3. Coconut			

	4. Areca nut 5. Others			
	Total			

4) Sources of irrigation:

1) Well	2) Canal	3) River	4) Bore well	5) Other
Total irrigated area:				

5) Irrigation Structure:

Type of irrigation	Year of construction	Purchase value (Rs.)	Present value (Rs.)	Area irrigated (ha)	Expenses on maintenance and repairs (Rs.)
Well a) Open b) Bore					
Electric motor with pump					
Pipeline					
Other					

6) Expenses incurred on irrigation Fuel/ Electricity and Water charges/ taxes

Diesel oil		Fuel oil/ Grease		Electricity charges	Water taxes	No. of irrigations
Qty (lit.)	(Rs.)	Qty (lit.)	(Rs.)	(Rs.)	(Rs.)	

7) Inventory of implements and farm machinery:

Sr.No.	Type	No.	Purchase price/unit (Rs.)	Present Value / Unit (Rs.)	Remaining life	Repairing charges
I.	Implements					
	a) Wooden Plough					

	b) Iron plough					
	c) harrow					
II.	Bullock cart					
III.	Machinery					
	a) Oil engine					
	b) Electric motor					
	c) Sprayer					
	d) Duster					
IV.	Others Hand Tools					
	a) Sickle					
	b) Axe					
	c) Spade					
	d) Koyta					
	e) Iron Basket					
	f) Plastic crates					
	g) Wooden barrel					
	h) Pick axe					
	i) Bucket					
	j) Others					

8) Inventory of buildings and other farm structures:

Particulars	Area (ha)	Year of Construction	Cost of Construction (Rs.)	Present value (Rs.)	Expected life (years)	Repairing cost (Rs.)
Residential Building						
Engine House						

Storehouse						
Cattle other						
Any other						

9) Inventory of livestock:

Sr. No.	Type	No.	Breed	Age (Years)	Owned/ Purchased	Present value (Rs.)
1)	Draft					
	a) Bullock					
	b) He-buffalo					
2)	Cow					
	a) In milk					
	b) Dry					
3)	Buffalo					
	a) In milk					
	b) Dry					
4)	Young stock (below 3 yrs.)					
	a) Cow					
	b) Buffalo					
5)	Sheep					
6)	Goats					
7)	Poultry					
8)	Others					

www.ingramcontent.com/pod-product-compliance
Lightning Source LLC
Chambersburg PA
CBHW040218110726
48005CB00019B/3066